Canterbury

Canterbury

Canterbury

Martin Andrew

Waterton Press Limited

First published in the United Kingdom in 1998 by
Frith Publishing an imprint of Waterton Press Limited.

British Library Cataloguing in Publication Data.

Martin Andrew
Canterbury

ISBN 1-84125-015-5

Reproductions of all the photographs in this book are available as framed or mounted prints. For more information please contact The Francis Frith Collection at the address below quoting the title of this book and the page number and photograph number or title.

The Francis Frith Collection,
PO Box 1697, Salisbury, Wilts SP3 5TW
Tel: 01747 855 669
E mail: bookprints@francisfrith.com

Typeset in Bembo

Printed and bound in Great Britain by
WBC Limited, Bridgend, Glamorgan.

Contents

Francis Frith 1822-1898

Introduction

Francis Frith: A Victorian Pioneer

Francis Frith, the founder of the world famous photographic archive was a complex and multitudinous man. A devout Quaker and a highly successful and respected Victorian businessman he was also a flamboyant character.

By 1855 Frith had already established a wholesale grocery business in Liverpool and sold it for the astonishing sum of £200,000, equivalent of over £15,000,000 today. Now a multi-millionaire he was able to indulge in his irresistible desire to travel. As a child he had poured over books penned by early explorers, and his imagination had been stirred by family holidays to the sublime mountain regions of Wales and Scotland. "What a land of spirit-stirring and enriching scenes and places!" he had written. He was to return to these scenes of grandeur in later years to "recapture the thousands of vivid and tender memories", but with a very different purpose. Now in his thirties, and captivated by the new science of photography, Frith set out on a series of pioneering journeys to the Middle East, that occupied him from 1856 until 1860.

He took with him a specially-designed wicker carriage which acted as camera, dark-room and sleeping chamber. These far-flung journeys were full of intrigue and adventure. In his life story, written when he was sixty-three, Frith tells of being held captive by bandits, and fighting "an awful midnight battle to the very point of exhaustion and surrender with a deadly pack of hungry, wild dogs.He bargained for several weeks with a "mysterious priest" over a beautiful seven-volume illuminated Koran, which is now in the British Museum. Wearing full arab costume, Frith arrived at Akaba by camel seventy years before Lawrence of Arabia, where he encountered "desert princes and rival sheikhs, blazing with jewel-hilted swords".

During these extraordinary adventures he was assiduously exploring the desert regions of the Nile and recording the antiquities and people with his camera, Frith was the first photographer ever to travel beyond the sixth cataract. Africa, we must remember, was still the "Dark Continent", and Stanley and Livingstone's famous meeting was a decade into the future. The conditions for picture taking confound belief. He laboured for hours on end in his dark-room in the sweltering heat, while the volatile collodion chemicals fizzed dangerously in their trays. Often he was forced to work in tombs and caves where conditions were cooler.

Back in London he exhibited his photographs and was "rapturously cheered" by the Royal in Society. His reputation as a photographer was made overnight. His photographs were issued in albums by James S. Virtue and William MacKenzie, and published simultaneously in London and New York. An eminent historian has likened their impact on the population of the time to that on our own generation of the first photographs taken on the surface of the moon.

Characteristically, Frith spotted the potential to create a new business as a specialist publisher of photographs. In 1860 he married Mary Ann Rosling and set out to photograph every city, town and village in Britain. For the next thirty years Frith travelled the country by train and by pony and trap, producing photographs that were keenly bought by the millions of Victorians who, because of the burgeoning rail network, were beginning to enjoy holidays and day trips to Britain's seaside resorts and beauty spots.

To meet the demand he gathered together a team of up to twelve photographers, and also published the work of independent artist-photographers of the reputation of Roger Fenton and Francis Bedford. Together with clerks and photographic printers he employed a substantial staff at his Reigate studios. To gain an understanding of the scale of Frith's business one only has to look at the catalogue issued by Frith & Co. in 1886. It runs to some 670 pages listing not only many thousands of views of the British Isles but also photographs of most major European countries, and China, Japan, the USA and Canada. By 1890 Frith had created the greatest specialist photographic publishing company in the world.

He died in 1898 at his villa in Cannes, his great project still growing. His sons, Eustace and Cyril, took over the task, and Frith & Co. continued in business for another seventy years, until by 1970 the archive contained over a third of a million pictures of 7,000 cities, towns and villages.

The photographic record he has left to us stands as a living monument to a remarkable and very special man.

Frith's dhow in Egypt *c.*1857

Chapter 1

The City of Canterbury
Pilgrims to a Walled City

Although visitors and modern day pilgrims come to Canterbury Cathedral from all over the world, the city itself has an extraordinarily rich survival of historic buildings: timber-framed, stone, brick and flint; medieval, Tudor, seventeenth century, Georgian and Victorian. This is despite the infamous fire bombing of the city in the Baedeker Raid of 1 June 1942 which destroyed 10 per cent of the city centre and further civil destructions after the War in the name of 'progress'. Fortunately the architectural heritage of the city is now recognised and actively promoted. For much of the year the city is packed with tourists and visitors, a high proportion of them French and often school parties.

There was already a pre-Roman settlement at this crossing of the River Stour, but it was the Roman Conquest which transformed this trade centre into the walled city of *Cantiacorum Durovernum* soon after AD 43 with its own huge amphitheatre and forum. The Cantii tribe live on in the county name of Kent which makes it the oldest county name in England. The Roman city was walled and had the classic cross of main streets, one completely unchanged in its route, comprising St Peter Street, High Street and St George Street, the other more changed and diverted, running from Castle Street but diverted around the cathedrals precincts. Canterbury played a key part in the Roman provinces communications network, being at the junction of three roads, including Watling Street.

Canterbury had a vital role in the return of Christianity to England after the Romans left, and St Augustine's arrival in AD 597 is one of the dates every school child knows. Indeed the medieval city owed most of its prosperity over and above its county town and market functions to the cathedral, the seat of the Archbishops of Canterbury, and for the years after the Murder of Archbishop Thomas à Becket in 1170, to its pre-eminent pilgrimage role, immortalised in Chaucer's *Canterbury Tales*. Much of its fine circuit of medieval walls and towers survive, some on Roman foundations.

Pilgrimage brought great wealth but the Reformation of the sixteenth century ended the veneration of saints, and the city, after Puritan turbulence, settled down to being the county town, a market centre and an important coaching town on the way to France.

In the eighteenth century there was much rebuilding and unfortunately even then, highway improvements were destructive: three of the four great medieval gateways were demolished. However to some extent the long quiet centuries preserved the fabric of the city and it entered the twentieth century remarkably intact.

(C18061)

The Cathedral and city from the air, *c.*1935.
Then, as now, the cathedral dominates the city. Many of the foreground buildings were destroyed in the 1942 blitz and by the later ring road.

(C18003)

A city view, *c.*1955.
Beyond the chimneypots and roofs of the ancient city, loom the white walls of the Odeon of 1933 (now the Marlowe Theatre) and the mighty cathedral.

(C18022)

The Butter Market, *c.*1955.
Our exploration of the city starts in the Butter Market, a small square surrounded by jettied medieval buildings at the gateway to the cathedral.

(C18027)

Mercery Lane, *c.*1955.
The buildings on the left side of this fine medieval street were once the Chequers Inn, built about 1390 for pilgrims to the shrine of St Thomas à Becket.

(C18079)

The High Street, *c.*1955.
Following the line of the Roman main axis, the High Street leads towards Westgate. The jettied buildings on the right flank Mercery Lane.

(70331a)

Old Weavers House, 1921.
Built in 1561, the weavers in the name were Flemish refugees. The gables and oriels overlooking the tranquil River Stour badly needed repair in 1921.

(C18065)

The River Stour, *c.*1955.
Looking east from the bridge in The Friars, the tranquil scene now has fewer trees. On the right is the corner of the Blackfriars' thirteenth century refectory.

(C18104)

Old Weavers House, *c.*1955.
Seen from Eastbridge where the Stour passes under the High Street, by this time the building has been carefully restored.

(C18063)

Old Weavers House from the east, *c.*1955.
Beyond the Old Weavers House and Eastbridge, the battlements are part of Eastbridge Hospital, founded in 1180 for poor pilgrims.

(70328)

St Peter's Street, 1921.
Amid the medieval gables, the tall house on the right is a timbered house clad in 'mathematical tiles', hanging tiles that look like bricks.

G.H.HEATH
G.H.HEATH
WHO ESA
& RITAIL
TOBACCONIST.
CONFECTIONER
IST & CONFECTIONE

(C18041)

St Peter's Street, 1951.
Looking towards Westgate, the last surviving medieval city gate built in 1375-81. There's still remarkably little traffic in the 1950s.

(C18088)

Westgate from Westgate Gardens, *c.*1955.
The drum towers of Westgate seen beyond an archway which led through the medieval city wall onto a bridge, now long gone.

(C18018)

Westgate Gardens and Tower House, *c.*1955.
Beyond the remains of the bridge is Tower House, once a tower on the city wall. A popular spot for eating lunchtime sandwiches.

(70330)

Westgate from St Dunstan's Street, 1921.
One of the finest streets in the city is outside its walls. A fine view of the Westgate which also had a drawbridge over the river.

(70333)

Dane John, 1921.
The park donated to the city by Alderman Simmons in 1790 was on the site of the castle or 'donjon'. The fountain and bandstand have now gone.

(76111)

Grey Friars, 1924.
Accessible from Stour Street this picturesque friary building of about 1267 spans a branch of the Stour.

(40848)

St John's Hospital Gateway, Northgate, 1898.

This ancient hospital glimpsed through the gates, was founded by Archbishop Lanfranc before 1100, but the gateway itself dates from about 1600.

(21407a)

The Great Gateway or Fyndon Gate, St Augustine's Abbey, Lady Wootton's Green, 1888.
Built between 1300-1309 by Abbot Fyndon, this fine gateway led in to the abbey founded by St.Augustine in AD 598 beyond the city walls.

(3383)

St Martin's Church, St Martin's Hill, *c.*1866.
On a hill to the east of the city, this church may predate St Augustine's arrival in AD 597. The distant cathedral is now only glimpsed between the trees.

(3384)

St Martin's Churchyard walls, *c.*1866.
The church is now even more obscured by trees, but the flint wall remains.

(40851)

Queen Bertha's Tomb in St Martin's Church, 1898.
Bertha was the Christian wife of King Ethelbert of Kent who was converted by St Augustine. Unfortunately the tomb when opened, contained the bones of an old man!

Chapter 2

Canterbury Cathedral
'The principal object of admiration'

Because Kent was first recovered for Christianity after the Anglo-Saxon (and Jutish) conquest of much of England, the capital of the Jutish kingdom, the old Roman city now named Cantwarabyrig, was in the right place at the right time. St Augustine decided that Christchurch, which he had founded in AD 602 would become the seat of the Archbishop, the Primate of All England, and thus it has remained.

This importance is to be seen in the cathedral itself, which is an architectural tour de force of great power and appeal. Architecturally it is like an onion with layers from every period of medieval architecture. After the Norman Conquest of 1066 the first Norman Archbishop, Lanfranc, demolished the Saxon buildings and built a new cathedral in the 1070s. Parts of his cathedral are buried in the walls of the transept and the nave north wall and, remarkably, the great central tower, known as Bell Harry, is carried on Lanfranc's crossing tower piers, admittedly encased in later work.

The next layer of the onion is the crypt and choir outer walls, the east transept and side chapels which date from Priors Ernulf and Conrad's rebuilding of Lanfranc's choir. Between 1096 and 1130 they greatly enlarged the church eastwards beyond the crossing.

So things remained until 1170, when the Archbishop, Thomas à Becket, was murdered in the north transept by four knights, zealously misinterpreting one of Henry II's tantrums. This murder rocked Christendom and Thomas was rapidly elevated to sainthood in 1173.

Conveniently, the choir burned down the next year and gave a golden opportunity to provide a fitting setting for Thomas' shrine. The inside of the burnt-out choir was demolished and a Frenchman, William of Sens, designed the new Gothic work. Unfortunately he fell from the scaffolding and William the Englishman took over in 1179. The choir has a wasp waisted effect through the retention of the Norman shell, but this adds to its architectural power and the choir must be one of the finest church interiors in the country.

The nave was rebuilt in Perpendicular style (1391-1405), probably by Henry Yevele, the King's architect. The final crowning element, the marvellous central tower, Bell Harry, was added in 1494-1503, designed by the king's then architect, John Wastell. Lanfranc's original north-west tower of the nave survived until the 1830s, by which time it was dangerous and was rebuilt as a copy of the south-west tower.

It is not possible to do more than convey a little of the magnificent quality of the cathedral, and I hope the photographs that follow capture some of the essence. As Erasmus said in the sixteenth century: "The great church rears itself to the sky so majestically that it strikes us with religious awe even from a distance".

(5288)

Canterbury Cathedral from the south-west, *c.*1870.
Seen from the top of the Christchurch Gate entrance to the precincts, the great cathedral has changed little since 1870.

(21353)

Canterbury cathedral from the west, 1888.
This unusual view above the rooftops shows how closely the left-hand tower, rebuilt in the 1830s, copied the original.

(25679)

Canterbury Cathedral west towers from Christchurch Gate, 1890.
The building on the left still sells guide books. Note the scaffolding or 'putlog' holes that pepper the tower.

(C18051)

Canterbury Cathedral from Christchurch Gate, *c.*1955.
This modern view shows how the pinnacles and turrets sweep the building skyward, climaxing with Bell Harry, the great central tower.

(21354)

Canterbury Cathedral choir from the east, 1888.
Astonishingly, the Corona chapel on the right was left unfinished from 1184 until the 1740s when the battlements were added.

(25682)

Canterbury Cathedral. The Norman Tower to the south-east transept, 1890.
Prior Ernulf's richly decorated early twelfth century towers give some idea of the quality before the fire in 1147.

(21399)

Canterbury Cathedral. Norman arcading on the outside of the choir, 1888.
Prior Ernulf's blind arcading with the arches intersecting, produces the type of complex decorative pattern so popular with Norman masons.

(21357)

Canterbury Cathedral from the north, 1888.
From the well-tended rose garden to Walpole House, this more distant view shows how Bell Harry tower majestically dominates the cathedral.

(25675)

Canterbury Cathedral. Bell Harry Tower, 1890.
From the Deanery garden the soaring pinnacles flank two tiers of long elegant openings, the upper being the cathedral belfry.

(40845)

Canterbury Cathedrals Norman Crypt, 1898.
This wonderful atmospheric space dates from the early twelfth century. The elegant fourteenth century stone screens enclose the Chapel of our Lady of the Undercroft.

(21396)

Canterbury Cathedrals Norman Crypt looking east, 1888.
Prior Ernulf's columns have plain shafts and carved capitals or vice versa. On the right-hand carved column, a careless mason started to carve the capital.

(40844)

Canterbury Cathedrals Norman Crypt looking west, 1889.
The elegant arcades and vaults supporting the choir pavement above, have thankfully now lost the heating pipes across the distant bays.

(21392)

Canterbury Cathedral. The Trinity or Eastern Crypt, 1888.
This eastern part of the crypt dates from the 1180's and supports the pavement of William the Englishman's eastern Trinity Chapel.

(25692)

Canterbury Cathedral. The Trinity or Eastern Crypt, 1890.
Two years later, stones are piled on the floor during repair work. The two decayed marble columns subsequently had to be renewed.

(25689)

Canterbury Cathedral. The Transept of the Martyrdom, 1890.
Thomas à Becket was murdered here, below the (later) memorial. This has now been moved and replaced by a modern alter and sculpture.

(25688a)

Canterbury Cathedrals Choir looking east, 1890.
Taking a mere decade to build, this wonderful late twelfth century space climbs to the high altar with its Victorian re-redos.

(70340)

Canterbury Cathedrals Choir, 1921.
By 1921 the reredos have gone and the full glory of the choir with its smooth limestone and dark Purbeck marble shafting can be appreciated.

(25691)

Canterbury Cathedral. St Augustine's Chair, 1890.
For centuries placed in the Corona or east chapel, this thirteenth century Purbeck marble chair may replace a much earlier one, perhaps even St Augustine's.

(21377)

Canterbury Cathedral. The Trinity Chapel from the ambulatory, 1888.
The eastern arm of the choir was the site of St Thomas à Becket's Shrine, which was destroyed in 1538 on Henry VIII's orders.

(21379)

Canterbury Cathedral: The Tomb of the Black Prince, 1888.
Victor of Crécy and Poitiers, the great soldier prince's armour still hangs above him, while he lies in the copper gilt effigy below.

(21382a)

Canterbury Cathedral: Archbishop Tait's Monument, north-east transept, 1888.

The archbishop, who died in 1882, lies in a superbly carved marble effigy, upon a tomb chest richly inlaid with coloured marbles and granites.

(21383)

Canterbury Cathedral: The Warriors. Chapel in the south-west transept, 1888.

Originally a fourteenth century chantry chapel, it now commemorates the fallen in war, particularly Kent regiments, and is now hung with battle-scarred flags.

(1076)

Canterbury Cathedral Nave looking east, *c.*1862.
Henry Yevele's great nave of 1391-1405 is uncluttered in 1862, and has no nave altar below the distant crossing arches.

(21367)

Canterbury Cathedral Nave looking west, 1888.
Yevele emphasised the nave's narrowness and relative height by a forest of slender shafts rising to an elegantly patterned lierne vault above.

(40840)

Canterbury Cathedral Nave looking east, 1898.

Bell Harry's lantern sheds light at the far end. The pulpit was brand new, having been installed in the year this photograph was taken.

Chapter 3

Canterbury Cathedral Precincts
The Priory of Christ Church and The King's School

The cathedral sits in the middle of a monastery, whose ruins are all around. These precincts were walled and entered by two great gateways, Christchurch Gate through which all paying customers enter from the Butter Market and the Court Gatehouse into the King's School Green Court. The north and east boundary of the priory was formed by the Romans and then the city walls were rebuilt in the Middle Ages. Within the walled precincts the Benedictine monks lived, disturbed only by countless thousands of pilgrims to the jewelled shrine of the martyred archbishop, Thomas à Becket.

The cathedral was not fully monastic until about AD 1000, when Archbishop Aelfric expelled the married clergy and replaced them by monks. Lanfranc, after the Norman Conquest, reformed the setup into a Benedictine Cathedral-Priory and thus it remained until the Dissolution of the Monasteries under Henry VIII, Canterbury being dissolved in March 1539. After this, it was run by a Dean and Chapter, as it is to this day. Architecturally the consequence of the dissolution was much more demolition of priory buildings.

However, a surprising amount of Norman work remains, although only part of it from Lanfranc's period, and the bulk from his Norman successors up to about 1160. Later, Priors remodelled and extended, or rebuilt, but Norman arches enriched with chevron carving and other mouldings can be seen everywhere. Astonishingly, a plan of the priory drawn in about 1165 survives, which shows the cathedral and priory buildings with considerable accuracy, although not to scale. Many are recognisable, including the Norman Staircase and water tower, the cloisters, the infirmary, the Court Gate and other buildings. This survival is quite remarkable and unique. Although it was drawn principally to show the piped water system and drains, its value to those interested in architecture is priceless, and is perhaps the oldest surviving ground plan in England.

Although the bombs in June 1942 missed most of the cathedral, they did damage to the monastic buildings north of the cathedral. Much of this has been repaired but it shows how lucky Canterbury and England were that the cathedral survived. Nowadays, modern pilgrims and visitors are not confined to Green Court and the area between Christchurch Gate and the cathedral doors, so we can get some feel of the secret world of this priory of vast wealth and influence. It must be remembered as well, that the tranquil ruins give a misleading impression of the bad relations between the archbishops and the monks that bedevilled the centuries before the Dissolution.

(329)

Canterbury Cathedral. Christchurch Gate, *c.*1860.
This early photograph shows the state of the great gateway of 1517-21, its panelled and carved stonework crumbling away to dust.

(21407)

Canterbury Cathedral. Christchurch Gateway into the precincts, 1888.

Besides decaying steadily, the gateway lost its niche statue of Christ to Puritans in the seventeenth century and its corner turrets in the eighteenth.

(C18052)

Canterbury Cathedral. Christchurch Gate, *c.*1955.
Following restoration by the Friends of Canterbury Cathedral in the 1930s, the gate regained its corner turrets and architectural quality.

(76106)

Canterbury Cathedral from the War Memorial Gardens, 1924.
Occupying the site of the convent gardens, this tranquil World War I memorial garden is entered through a relocated Norman archway.

(5292)

Canterbury Cathedral. Ruins of the Infirmary and its Chapel, *c.*1870.
Beyond the chapel nave arch, the south arcade of about 1100 was saved by being incorporated into a fifteenth century house for the Sub-Prior, now removed.

(21388)

Canterbury Cathedral Cloisters, the south walk, 1888.
The Norman cloisters were rebuilt under Prior Chillenden around 1400, the elegant lierne vaults incorporating over eight hundred heraldic bosses.

(21387)

Canterbury Cathedral Cloisters. The entrance from the Transept of the Martyrdom, 1888.
The richly carved thirteenth century arches and doorway are obscured by Prior Chillenden's vaulting and shafts, but few visitors notice.

(21389)

Canterbury Cathedral Cloisters north walk, 1888.
More decay and missing stonework. The two open arches led into the lavatorium where the monks washed before eating.

(21361)

Canterbury Cathedral Cloisters East Walk, 1888.
Behind the cloister walk is the vast chapter house west window and the remains of the Norman dormitory, topped by the wheel-windowed Neo-Norman library.

(21365)

Canterbury Cathedral. The Dark Entry or The Black Walk, 1888.
Much overgrown and ruinous, this walkway linked the more open Green Court with the closed world of the monks. It is now restored.

(21358a)

Canterbury Cathedral. The North Gate from Green Court, 1888.
This creeper-clad fifteenth century gateway linked the private world of the monks with Green Court via the Black Walk behind. The trees have long gone.

(70336)

Canterbury Cathedral. The North Gate from beside the Deanery, 1921.
Prior Selling's gatehouse has been restored and the trees replaced by railings. A corner of the rambling Deanery is on the left.

(25674)

Canterbury Cathedral. Bell Harry tower from the Deanery garden, 1890.
Picturesque creeper-choked ruins flank the Black Walk and form a backdrop to the Dean's Victorian garden beds and tubs.

(6197)

Canterbury Cathedral from the Deanery garden, *c.*1872.
The cathedral is about the only building not covered in creeper in this view from further back in the Dean's garden.

(C18060)

Canterbury Cathedral. New Court and the King's School War Memorial, *c.*1955.
The ancient school, with an unbroken line of headmasters recorded since 1291, occupies most of the buildings around Green Court.

(76107)

Canterbury Cathedral. The Aula Nova and the Norman Stair, 1924. The North Hall, a third of the nine bay hall Prior Wibert raised in the 1150s, retains its Norman undercroft and external roofed staircase.

(21401)

Canterbury Cathedral. The Norman Stair, 1888.

A rare survival, this staircase can be seen on the 1160s plan of the priory, itself a remarkable link back to Norman times.

Chapter 4

Around Canterbury. Villages along the Great Stour River: Fordwich, Sturry and Chartham.

The map of Kent has changed greatly since medieval times, when the Isle of Thanet was indeed an island cut off from the mainland by the Wantsum Channel that ran from Sandwich to Reculver. An estuary ran west towards Canterbury, and Fordwich, 2 miles east of Canterbury, was its thriving port, in effect at the mouth of the River Great Stour. Caen limestone from Normandy and Purbeck marble from Dorset, were shipped here for the cathedral building works. So important was Fordwich that it was allowed to join the Cinque Ports as a Corporate Member to Sandwich. These medieval Cinque Ports supplied ships for the king's fleet in wartime, in return for various tax and other privileges.

However, the Wantsum Channel silted steadily until by the sixteenth century ships could no longer reach Fordwich, and the river became much as it is today and the island nature of the Isle of Thanet a mere memory. Fordwich, though now more like a peaceful village, claims to be England's smallest town. Having a mayor from 1292 until 1883, its ceremonial maces are now in Canterbury Museum, and it has a town hall, a not very large fifteenth century timber-framed building jettied on all four sides.

Less than half a mile north of Fordwich, on the north bank of the Great Stour is Sturry, a village that had its origins at the river crossing of the Roman road east from Canterbury. Sturry suffered horribly during the war when a parachute mine hit the centre of the village on 14 November 1941, obliterating the High Street and killing seventeen people, including four members of the Johncock family.

The third village in this chapter is on the other side of Canterbury where the Great Stour cuts through the chalk Downs in a wide, flat valley from Ashford to Canterbury. The village centre is dominated by the Chartham Paper Mill which developed from a village corn mill during the nineteenth century into one specialising in the manufacture of tracing paper. Its Victorian buildings were demolished or refronted after the Second World War when the company secured confiscated German paper-making machinery: the revamped buildings proudly display this date of '1949'. The village itself has had much rebuilding and new housing, but its core is still evident. The former county mental asylum, St Augustine's Hospital, dominant on the hills south of the village is now closed, and its site is being developed for new housing as 'Chartham Downs' with some old buildings retained and converted.

(40854)

FORDWICH. The Town Hall and Dipping Chair, 1898.
Inside "the smallest town in England's" town hall, a fine timber-framed and jettied building, open from May to September and at Easter.

(44224)

STURRY. St Nicholas' Parish Church from the south, 1899.
The iron fence and the conifers have now gone, but otherwise this view of the church with its good, plain Norman west tower is unchanged.

(44223)

Parish Church and Milner Court Gate Arch, STURRY, 1899.
The mellow Tudor brick archway led to Sir Thomas Smythe's mansion of 1583, Milner Court, now the junior department of King's School, Canterbury.

(44220)

Sturry High Street and Post Office, 1899.
Only the most distant buildings survived the parachute bomb that fell in November 1941: it has all been rebuilt.

(44225)

STURRY. The Bridge over the River Great Stour, 1899.
This eighteenth century bridge spans a branch of the river which powered the nearby watermill, now demolished, although the mill house survives.

(50355)

CHARTHAM. St Mary's Parish Church from the south-east, 1903.
A wonderful decorated Gothic style church with superb 'Kentish' window tracery, built in the decades either side of 1300. It is usually locked.

(50354)

CHARTHAM. St Mary's Parish Church from The Green, 1903.
The houses left of the church were demolished about 1910, but one replacement is called Bakery House to commemorate its predecessor.

(50353)

CHARTHAM. The Green, north side 1903.
Bedford House, on the right, now has its fine timber-framing exposed and the hipped-roofed single storey smithy building survives to its left.

(60304)

CHARTHAM. Riverside from the railway bridge over the Great Stour, 1908.
The house and cottage beyond have gone, replaced by a yellow brick Riverside House of about 1914. The corner building survives.

(53461)

CHARTHAM. The Great Stour and the railway bridge and crossing, 1906.
Oast Cottage at the left is medieval with seventeenth century brickwork. Riverside Gatehouse beyond, was the railway crossing gatekeeper's cottage.

(50358)

CHARTHAM. Great Stour Bridge from the south, 1903.
The trees on the right have gone, and are replaced by modern houses and gardens, but the bridge of 1857 remains.

(53463)

CHARTHAM. The Great Stour looking east towards the Village, 1906.
This attractive view is unchanged and gives a good idea of the flat valley the river has cut through the chalk Downs.

(53458)

CHARTHAM. The Parade looking north, 1905.
The paper mill is behind the photographer. Mill workers eat their sandwiches in the field on the right, now a recreation ground.

(60309)

CHARTHAM. The Paper Mill from the weir, looking west, 1908.
The mill and the millworkers' cottages on the right in this view are now completely hidden by trees.

(50357)

CHARTHAM Paper Mill, 1903.
This long mid-nineteenth century mill building survives under colourwashed render on brick and with an extra storey, all prominently dated '1949'.

(51045)

Chartham Paper Mill and The Grange, 1903.
The tracing paper mill buildings have been greatly enlarged in recent years, and the brick chimney has gone, to be replaced by steel ones.

(60307)

CHARTHAM. The Grange, 1908.
Built about 1860, The Grange is reached via the mill's access and its outlook south is dominated by modern mill buildings.

(53457)

CHARTHAM. The Deanery and Nickholt from the south, 1906.
The Deanery, on the left, is an eighteenth century house but nothing to do with Canterbury's Dean. Sadly, the oast houses no longer exist.

(51044)

CHARTHAM. Horton Chapel from the west, 1903.
This fourteenth century former chapel cannot now be seen in this view, the trees having grown taller. The oasts have also gone.

(53464)

CHARTHAM. St Augustine's Hospital from the Garling Green road, 1906.
The old County Lunatic Asylum fills the horizon in this tranquil scene. No child would sensibly push a pram along a Kent road nowadays.

(50359)

CHARTHAM. St Augustine's Hospital entrance gates and Lodge looking east, 1903.
The scale of the former asylum can be seen in this view past the lodge and the Chartham entrance gates, the latter now demolished and the hospital closed.

(50360)

CHARTHAM. St Augustine's Hospital, 1903.
The main block, fortunately retained in the current housing scheme, shows the quality of John Giles and Gough's 1872 competition winning design.

(50362)

CHARTHAM. Shalmsford Bridge and wagon wash, 1903.
Rebuilt to cope with traffic to the asylum in 1876 by the County Surveyor, the bridge incorporated 1711 date stones from the earlier bridge.

(50361)

CHARTHAM. The mill on the Great Stour from the east, 1903.
This former corn mill can be seen from the A28 opposite the cemetery, but it is no longer functional.

(53462)

CHARTHAM. River Great Stour, Dabchick, 1906.
The beauty of the Great Stour river in its chalk valley is brought out well in this tranquil scene.

Chapter 5

Around Canterbury. Villages on the Little Stour river and the Nail Bourne, Wickhambreux, Ickham, Littlebourne and Bridge.

The Little Stour river is a much less grand affair than the Great Stour. Rising near Lyminge, a mere five miles from the English Channel, it heads north through the chalk of the Downs as the Nail Bourne, becoming the Little Stour at Littlebourne. Until the later Middle Ages it, like the Great Stour, had been much wider, silted up to its present size but still sufficient to power numerous water mills such as those at Littlebourne, Seaton and Wickhambreux.

Wickhambreux or known locally as Wickham, the - breux suffix being a corrupted version of 'Briouse', the Norman family who held the manor, has a fine green, somewhat overwhelmed by its white-painted weatherboarded watermill. The river then winds a little further downstream to Seaton where it powers another mill, which is now in Ickham parish.

Ickham village itself is not quite on the river, its main street starting about 300 yards away. The village has some good farmhouses and minor gentry houses. There are several examples of the Dutch and Flemish influenced gable ends, usually in thin red brick imported in the seventeenth and eighteenth centuries as return cargoes from Dutch brick pits into Kent, East Anglia and Lincolnshire.

Upstream we reach the much larger village of Littlebourne with its busy through road. I asked in a village shop if there was a guide to the village: she laughed and said Littlebourne was much too small to have had anything ever happen of interest! Well, it has a most attractive green, a good church and some fine houses and villagescape. To the east is Lee Priory, once one of England's most interesting Gothick Revival houses. Designed by Samuel Wyatt and built in the 1780s for a friend of Horace Walpole of Strawberry Hill fame, it was drastically remodelled by George Gilbert Scott in the 1860s and demolished after the War: only Scott's stables remain converted to a house.

South-west past the Well Chapel ruins, we reach Bridge, now mercifully by-passed. Here are or were three mansions close to the old Roman road to Dover and in more rolling countryside: Bifrons, now demolished, Bridge Place, brick-built for Sir Arnold Braems after 1638 in a pure Classical style but now much reduced in size, and Bourne Park, an early eighteenth century mansion set in fine parkland. George Gilbert Scott did extraordinary things to the parish church and the workhouse of 1836 has been splendidly converted to twenty-six houses.

(49420)

WICKHAMBREUX. The Green, 1903.
The mill cottages on the left fix this northerly view across the green: now almost treeless, well-manicured and not a sheep to be seen.

(51047)

Wickhambreux Court, The Green, 1903. This elegant house of about 1820 with its pretty green shutters has a yellow brick façade but the back and sides are in cheaper red brick.

(49426)

WICKHAMBREUX, The Willows, now Old Willows Farm, 1903.
Trees now largely obscure this attractive eighteenth century house, hiding behind its refined early Victorian rendered façades and bow windows.

(W92012)

WICKHAMBREUX. Post Office, now The Old Stone House, *c*.1955.
With its medieval chequerwork walls topped by crow step gables of about 1500, the house faces the weather-boarded mill with its great water wheel.

(49436)

Seaton Mill, Ickham from the west, 1903.
The mill remains converted to two houses, but has lost its upper storeys, steam engine chimney and the header pond has been infilled.

(49437)

Seaton Mill, Ickham from the east, 1903.
The mill, built as a cornmill but latterly a rubber factory, peers through the trees with the mill race to the left.

(I1026)

ICKHAM. The Old Rectory, *c.*1960.
The left-hand wing, shaded by the cedar, is a late thirteenth century house and a remarkable survival.

(I1027)

ICKHAM. The Forge and street, *c.*1960.
The farm building on the left has gone now, but the forge on the right, Ickham Engineering, still appears to be in use.

(49434)

ICKHAM. St John the Evangelist Parish Church from the south, 1903.
The thatched barn now has a shingled roof and a lychgate was built in 1919 as a war memorial.

(I1004)

ICKHAM. Pond Corner, *c.*1955.
Ickham Hall, a Regency house with an elegant columned porch and beyond the shuttered windows of Ickham Lodge, has now disappeared behind trees.

(I1019)

Littlebourne Mill, on the Wickhambreux road, *c.*1955.
This nineteenth century Little Stour watermill has been preserved by being converted to an attractive house.

(49430)

LITTLEBOURNE. St Vincent Parish Church from the south-east, 1903.
Kent had many vineyards in the Middle Ages and the dedication to St Vincent of Saragossa, patron saint of Vinedressers, echoes this.

(51055)

LITTLEBOURNE. Parish Church Lychgate, 1903.
The memorial lychgate was built in 1892, while to the left is the sweeping thatch roof of a massive fourteenth century aisled barn.

(49429)

LITTLEBOURNE. Church Road looking west, 1903.
A distant view of the church steeple from the junction with Nargate Street. The right-hand house has now been replaced.

(51053)

LITTLEBOURNE. Nargate Street looking north, 1903.
The road had a far more rural feel then, as it passes the gates to the grounds of Old Hall.

(L56301)

LITTLEBOURNE. Nargate Street looking towards The Square, *c.*1903.
The timber-framed building beyond Brewery House was part of the local brewery and is now turned into a house.

(49427)

LITTLEBOURNE. The High Street looking west, 1903.
All the buildings and oasthouses on the left have been demolished, but on the right all but the trees remain.

(L56019)

LITTLEBOURNE. The High Street looking west, *c.*1960.
The oasthouses on the left were still there in the 1960s. Note the 1930s telephone kiosk outside the post office.

POST OFFICE

(L56016)

LITTLEBOURNE. The War Memorial Hall, High Street, *c.*1960.
This somewhat stark hall was built in 1955, as a memorial to the service of the people of Littlebourne in two World Wars.

(51052)

LITTLEBOURNE. The Anchor Inn, The Square, 1903.
The inn has a Dutch gable on the right and this peaceful scene is now heavily tarmaced and traffic choked.

(49428)

LITTLEBOURNE. The King William IV and Littlebourne House, The Square, 1903.
The eighteenth century pub has lost its trees and Littlebourne House beyond is now a residential home and more visible than in this view.

(L56009)

LITTLEBOURNE. The Green, *c.*1960.
The trees still cast their shade. Littlebourne House in the distance shows off the porch added in 1938.

(51054)

LITTLEBOURNE. The Green, 1903.
The charming seventeenth century row of cottages have Dutch gables at each end, and Littlebourne House hides behind a high wall and gateway.

(L56022)

LITTLEBOURNE. The Green. Oast Houses and the Little Stour, *c.*1965.
Children play on a hot Summer's day beside the oast houses which survive, although partially obscured by an injudicious conifer.

(49431)

LITTLEBOURNE. The Bridge over the Little Stour, 1903.
While the ford is still there, the bridge has been rebuilt to carry the modern heavy traffic using this old Roman road.

(L56012)

LITTLEBOURNE. Lee Priory, *c.*1955.
Samuel Wyatt's 1780s Gothic house was heavily Victorianised in the 1860s and is seen here shortly before its demolition.

(49433)

LITTLEBOURNE. Lee Priory, 1903.
In peak condition in 1903, one can only see traces of the pretty Gothic house peeping through Scott's earnest Victorian remodelling.

(51056)

LITTLEBOURNE. The ruins of the Well Chapel, 1903.
Off Bekesbourne Lane, west of the village, mysterious fourteenth century chapel ruins sit by a small mere whose springs feed the Nail Bourne.

(51057)

BRIDGE. Bifrons Park: The Cascade, 1903.
The mansion was demolished by the Conynghams after the War and its elaborate water gardens and cascades are now mere archeological remains.

(49406)

BRIDGE. Laundry Lane (now Conyngham Lane),1903.
The estate laundry and cottage by the south-west entrance to Bifrons Park is seen in the distance. Modern housing replaces the trees on the right.

(49404)

BRIDGE. St Peter's Parish Church, 1903.
George Gilbert Scott introduced the huge Canterbury Cathedral scale capitals in the arcades in 1860 with mixed success, many feel.

(49405)

BRIDGE. From Church Meadows looking north-west, 1903.
Bridgeford House on the right is by a ford through the Nail Bourne. The windmill went in the 1960s to be replaced by housing.

(49408)

BRIDGE. Bourne Park, 1903.
Set in a landscaped park, this Queen Anne mansion built for the Auchers is in full public view from the Bourne Park Road.

(49407)

BRIDGE. Old England's Hole, 1903.
These are the remnant earthworks where, apparently, the Cantii made their last stand against the Roman Seventh Legion in AD 43.

1-84125 *Themed Poster Books* £4.99

000-7	Canals and Waterways	
001-5	High Days and Holidays	
003-1	Lakes and Rivers	
004-x	Piers	
005-8	Railways	
044-9	Ships	
002-3	Stone Circles & Ancient Monuments	
007-4	Tramcars	

Town & City Series £9.99

010-4	Brighton & Hove	
015-5	Canterbury	
012-0	Glasgow & Clydeside	
011-2	Manchester	
040-6	York	

Town & City series Poster Books £5.99

018-x	Around Brighton	
023-6	Canterbury	
043-0	Derby	
020-1	Glasgow	
011-2	Manchester	
041-4	York	

County Series £9.99

024-4	Derbyshire	
028-7	Kent	
029-5	Lake District	
031-7	Leicestershire	
026-0	London	
027-9	Norfolk	
030-9	Sussex	
025-2	Yorkshire	

County Series Poster Books £4.99

032-5	Derbyshire	
036-8	Kent	
037-6	Lake District	
039-2	Leicestershire	
034-1	London	
035-x	Norfolk	
038-4	Sussex	
033-3	Yorkshire	

Available soon

County Series £9.99

045-7	Berkshire	
053-8	Buckinghamshire	
055-4	East Anglia	
077-5	Greater London	
051-1	Lancashire	
047-3	Staffordshire	
049-x	Warwickshire	
063-5	West Yorkshire	

County Series Poster Books £4.99

046-5	Berkshire	
054-6	Buckinghamshire	
056-2	East Anglia	
078-3	Greater London	
052-x	Lancashire	
048-1	Staffordshire	
050-3	Warwickshire	
064-3	West Yorkshire	

Country Series £9.99

075-9	Ireland	
071-6	North Wales	
069-4	South Wales	
073-2	Scotland	

Country Series Poster Books £4.99

076-7	Ireland	
072-4	North Wales	
070-8	South Wales	
074-0	Scotland	

A selection of our 1999 programme:

County Series and Poster Books

Devon, Cornwall, Essex, Nottinghamshire, Cheshire.

Town and City Series and Poster Books

Bradford, Edinburgh, Liverpool, Nottingham, Stamford, Bristol, Dublin, Stratford-upon-Avon, Bath, Lincoln, Cambridge, Oxford, Matlock, Norwich.

Themed Poster Books

Castles, Fishing, Cricket, Bridges, Cinemas, The Military, Cars.